How To Get Your Life In Order

By

Ordering Your Life's Steps

SIMPLE IN 7 STEPS

How To Get Your Life In Order By Ordering Your Life's Steps

7 PRINCIPLES TO ACHIEVE PERSONAL GOALS

Dr. Jacki Edwards

XULON PRESS

Xulon Press
2301 Lucien Way #415
Maitland, FL 32751
407.339.4217
www.xulonpress.com

How To Get Your Life In Order By Ordering Your Life's Steps:
7 Principles to Achieve Personal Goals
© 2023 by Dr. Jacki Edwards

www.jackiedwards.me

All rights reserved solely by the author. The author guarantees all contents are original and do not infringe upon the legal rights of any other person or work. No part of this book may be reproduced in any form without the permission of the author.

Due to the changing nature of the Internet, if there are any web addresses, links, or URLs included in this manuscript, these may have been altered and may no longer be accessible. The views and opinions shared in this book belong solely to the author and do not necessarily reflect those of the publisher. The publisher therefore disclaims responsibility for the views or opinions expressed within the work.

Unless otherwise indicated, Scripture quotations taken from the King James Version (KJV)—*public domain.*

Paperback ISBN-13: 978-1-66286-615-9
Ebook ISBN-13: 978-1-66286-616-6

This book is dedicated in memory of my sister

SHERYL MARIE WHILBY

CONTENTS

MAKE CONSCIOUS DECISION
Page 1

SILENCE THE NOISE
Page 9

FOLLOW YOUR HEART
Page 17

EDUCATE YOURSELF
Page 25

UNDERSTAND YOUR WEAKNESS
Page 33

KNOW WHEN TO QUIT
Page 41

DISCOVER YOUR PURPOSE
Page 49

ABOUT THE AUTHOR
Page 57

Introduction

This self-development guide is based on the seven simple principles I have used in my own life to achieve my aspirations. These steps have helped me stay focused and resolute in my decisions to ultimately attain my goals. My accomplishments, whether academical, professional, or personal, all took place in small increments. My goals were not attained without struggles and hard work, and these seven steps kept me anchored throughout the process. With them, I achieved financial freedom, stability, peace of mind, and an unwavering relationship with my Creator.

Your journey may not be the same as mine, but maybe you are where I was before I intentionally changed the path my life was heading on. I felt that I was not living a life that was fulfilled or at full potential and was not where I wanted to be. Maybe you've made many broken promises to yourself and in the interim have developed self-doubt and uncertainty about reaching your personal goals. Whatever stage you are in, I believe this guidebook will help keep you on track to achieving the goals and visions you have for your life.

It is not too late to reach your full potential; the journey begins now. You have taken another chance on yourself, and this time, you will see "you" through the process. Believe that you are an overcomer, a conqueror, a winner, and a success story. You can reach your full potential and attain the dreams and goals you so desire. You have been given this simple tool that has been proven to get powerful results. Bet on yourself again and make your dreams become your reality.

STEP 1

MAKE CONSCIOUS DECISION

Make Conscious Decision

The moment you engage your mind in making a choice or decision, you immediately make a declaration of your desires to the unconscious mind. Once the subliminal part of your mind knows your aspirations, they will be reflected in your life. To be indecisive, on the other hand, not only creates weariness and worry but can also cloud the subconscious mind concerning what you want, where you desire to go, and what you wish to do. Conscious decision-making involves taking purposeful, intentional, and calculated steps with undivided attention to the task at hand. "It cannot be predicated on any other decisions. There are no "if's," "and's," or "but's" and no "What are they going to think or say?" thoughts. *(Do You Make Conscious or Unconscious Decisions?, 2014)*. Making a conscious decision is like a pregnant mom who realizes her baby is ready to make an entrance into the world. She begins to push without being concerned about being in the backseat of a car. She does not think of delaying the birth process until she arrives at the hospital. The decision is not attached to any foreseen circumstances other than that this baby needs to get out now.

Making a conscious decision has nothing to do with your past experiences or lack of resources. It is about making up your mind to act, move, go after, start over, do right, walk away, make a change, follow your dream, and walk into your purpose. The ups and downs of life and the circumstances and situations that are connected to life are unpredictable. This fact will never change. If you want to be successful and achieve your goals, you must become and remain flexible and adaptable to life's temper tantrums. You may have to tailor your plans or at times, redefine your purpose as you make the conscious choice to stay focused despite your current conditions. There may be times when the journey or path you decide to venture on gets lonely. You may even lose a friend or partner as you make the sound decision to go after your dreams. It is important to remember that this decision is personal and is influenced by your opinion, feelings, and desires.

It will take courage and confidence to move forward without hesitation, to the life you've envisioned, the dreams you've imagined, and the goals you wish to attain. That goal you desire will require your undivided attention, your deliberate actions, and your full awareness of each step of the journey. The power is within you! Make up your mind! Decide to decide!

> *"It is in the moment of decision that your destiny is shaped"*
> —Tony Robbins

Simple in 7 Steps Concept Application

STEP 1

MAKE CONSCIOUS DECISION

Conscious decision-making involves taking purposeful, intentional, and calculated steps with undivided attention to the task at hand. "It cannot be predicated on any other decisions." *(Do You Make Conscious or Unconscious Decisions?, 2014)*

List some examples of conscious and unconscious decisions you have made.

■ CONSCIOUS   ■ UNCONSCIOUS

_____   _____
_____   _____
_____   _____
_____   _____
_____   _____
_____   _____
_____   _____

Please list below some practical steps in making a conscious decision.

_____
_____
_____
_____
_____
_____

WHAT ARE YOUR GOALS?

The first step in making a conscious decision is to know what you want or desire to achieve. This section will help you identify your core desires and chart a way forward.

Write the goals you would like to achieve and why.

Goal:	Why it's important:
Goal:	Why it's important:
Goal:	Why it's important:
Goal:	Why it's important:

PRIORITIZE YOUR GOALS

In making a conscious decision, it is important to have a clear focus on one goal at a time. This will help you stay centered on all the aspects and processes of obtaining that goal.

In this section, you will prioritize the goals you created on the previous page. You will make the goal that you want to achieve first as #1 and so on.

Goal 1:

Goal 2:

Goal 3:

Goal 4:

Goal 5:

Goal 6:

STEP 2

SILENCE THE NOISE

Silence the Noise

Life is filled with many healthy and unhealthy distractions. A healthy distractor, for example, is taking a break from working to listen to your favorite music so you can relieve some stress. Removing yourself from a situation, even for a short period of time, can have long-term benefits to your overall well-being. In pursuit of your personal goals, an unhealthy distractor is anything or anyone that blurs your focal point and deters you from your goal. If that thing or person disturbs your flow or allows your concentration to deviate from your plans to reach your goals, then that distraction needs to be silenced. If it affects how you think, move, or proceed toward your dreams, it needs to be removed from your focus. Silencing the noise doesn't necessarily mean the sound completely dissipates or the distractor disappears. Rather, it means the distraction has faded into the background and become ineffective. As a result, you are no longer pulled away in the direction of the distraction.

To be effective in reaching your goals, a disconnection between you and any distractors must take precedence. Your goals can be negatively impacted if your environment is not conducive to where you want to go. Anything that does not align with your visions and goals will hinder and sabotage the outcome you want to achieve. The dynamics of life bring many uncertainties, and there will be times when situations may arise that must be dealt with immediately. It is important to remember that most distractions do not come from situations that require an urgent response, and many will resolve without your instant attention. It is imperative that you develop boundaries and skills that will help you stay focused on your goals and vision. The more you learn to ignore matters and people who are distractions, the more you will develop a strong-willed and determined mindset over them. You may have to mute that friend who doesn't share your goals by limiting conversations about your dreams and visions. That also applies to that family member who only dwells on the negative side of things. Sometimes you may have to tune out or turn off the television, phone, or any social media platforms that disrupt your attention to your goals.

Another big distraction to reaching your goal is your own negative thoughts. They can produce fear, discouragement, anxiety, and feelings of doubt. This will hinder your ability to take the first step toward achieving your goals and desires. Work diligently on pruning out the tares and weeds that tangle the garden of your mind and the progress you want to make in your life. Make positive affirmations every day about your health, mind, body, and desires. Spend quiet time alone to meditate and journal about the life you want. Take a step each day toward the goals and visions you have for your life, and most importantly, choose wisely what and who gets your undivided attention.

> "Don't let the noise of others' opinions drown your own inner voice."
> —Steve Jobs

Simple in 7 Steps Concept Application

STEP 2

SILENCE THE NOISE

Silencing the noise can be applied to anything that blurs your focal point. It can affect how you think, move, or proceed toward your aspirations.

How do distractions affect productivity?

_____
_____
_____
_____
_____

What are some common distractions that you have encountered?

_____
_____
_____
_____
_____

Write below how these distractions affected you from achieving your goals.

_____
_____
_____
_____
_____

In this section, list ways to minimize or remove these distractions for each of the categories below.

Things:

People:

Thoughts:

STEP 3

FOLLOW YOUR HEART

Follow Your Heart

In nursing school, I learned that the heart is the part of our anatomy that pumps blood throughout the entire body, carries oxygen and nutrients to our tissues, and removes carbon dioxide and other waste products to sustain life. Its rhythm creates electrical pulses that travel through our muscles and causes them to contract and pulsate. Just like the physical heart generates life in us, our inner voice gives us the impulse or motivation to act on our vision and dreams.

When our inner voice speaks to us, and we learn to act upon it, we give life to our senses, which energizes us to go after our dreams. We envision our life finally going in the right direction and start to feel that there is hope and the endless possibilities. Our inner voice is goal-directed and is a powerful guiding force to help pull us into the path we are destined for. Those burning desires will keep tugging and nudging until action is taken. In the physical heart, if blood flow ceases, death is imminent. In the same way, if we stop listening to the voice of our hearts, we are left feeling empty and unfulfilled.

Following your heart is not a "shatterproof" method. It doesn't guarantee that everything will be seamless and turn out the way you expected it, but in the end, you will feel the worth and satisfaction of acting on the desire within you. If there is dispassion or uncertainty, then you need to change your life's course and redirect it to where your heart is pointing. Living out your heart's aspirations and keeping first things first by focusing on what is essential in your life will lead you to a wave of inner peace. When you follow your heart, you will understand more about yourself and cultivate a renewed respect for who you are and who you are becoming.

Executing the desires of your heart can produce a life filled with meaning, fervency, and accomplishment. Listening to the voice of your heart can lead you into a life padded with passion, fulfillment, and purpose. Pay attention to those lingering thoughts about your goals, dreams, and aspirations. When we follow our hearts, we are simply doing what our internal mind or soul is telling us to do. Do not be afraid to take that leap of faith and step into the direction of your own God-given "Global Positioning System" (GPS). Follow the path that is designed specifically for you. Your destiny awaits you. It is time to begin the journey to the life your heart yearns for.

> *"Let yourself be silently drawn by the strange pull of what you really love. It will not lead you astray."*
> –Rumi

Simple in 7 Steps Concept Application

STEP 3

FOLLOW YOUR HEART

When you follow your heart, you will understand more about yourself and will cultivate a renewed respect for who you are and who you are becoming.

How do you differentiate the voice of the heart from that of the head?

_____
_____
_____
_____

What is your heart saying to you about your goals? What is your head saying to you about achieving your goals?

■ HEART	■ HEAD
_____	_____
_____	_____
_____	_____
_____	_____
_____	_____
_____	_____

What does it mean to follow your heart?

___

How do you know that you are following your heart?

___

How does your heart's desire align with your values?

___

STEP 4

EDUCATE YOURSELF

Educate Yourself

Education shapes how we think and operate and gives us leverage to achieve our life's goals and dreams. The modern world has become more complex with ever-changing innovation and technology. These forces stimulate us to grow, develop, and improve our knowledge and abilities. If we do not increase our capabilities and maintain a level of understanding, we will be at a disadvantage when trying to get to the next level in life. It is, therefore, vital to know the level of education you will need to aspire for the future you desire.

Whether it is formal, informal, or non-formal, education gives us the knowledge, new perspective, and opinions to understand the world we operate in. Formal education usually takes place in a school setting with qualified teachers as instructors. This type of education is planned with specific subjects and syllabi. Informal education may be a mother teaching her daughter how to brush her teeth or a dad teaching his son how to brush his hair. Informal education can also be gained by reading books or by gathering information from educational websites.

Non-formal education is performed outside of the normal educational or training institution. The learner usually makes the conscious decision to gather more skills or knowledge for personal growth and development. For example, community-based adult courses or practical/vocational education. Non-formal education can also take the form of continued education courses on the job or getting your certification for a particular skill. Education is a key element for learning and increasing the ability to interact with various individuals and situations and is an important tool used to improve one's life on many different levels. Take some time to assess your educational level for your dream job, the career change you want to make, and the pay grade you desire.

It is important to be open-minded to learning new things and ways as you continue to develop your path to success. Learning from the success strategies of others can also help to accelerate your own journey. Soliciting the helpful advice of those who have taken the road you are trying to walk is also essential in acquiring knowledge. It can be beneficial in preventing errors, circumventing difficulties, and obtaining insight or ideas to assist on the path to your destiny. Find the learning method that works best for you. Improve your mindset and skillset as deemed necessary to advance toward the life you have envisioned.

> *"Be a lifelong student. The more you learn, the more self-confidence you will have."*
> –Brian Tracy

Simple in 7 Steps Concept Application

STEP 4

EDUCATE YOURSELF

Education shapes the way we think and operate and gives us leverage to achieving our life's goals and dreams. It is vital to know the level of education you will need to aspire for the future you desire.

What type of learner are you? (Visual, Auditory, Kinesthetic, Read/Write).

☐ VISUAL   ☐ KINESTHETIC

☐ AUDITORY   ☐ READ/WRITE

In what ways does your learning style align with your educational goal?

_____

_____

_____

_____

_____

_____

_____

_____

_____

_____

SKILLS NEEDED TO ACHIEVE YOUR GOAL

Step 1: List the education needed to achieve your goals.

Step 2: Place F-formal, I-informal, and N-non-formal next to the education you will need for each goal.

EDUCATIONAL NEEDS	TYPE OF EDUCATION

EDUCATIONAL REQUIREMENT

Within each educational requirement, there are steps to be accomplished. List each of the steps required for the educational skill you will need in order to reach your goal.

☐ _____

☐ _____

☐ _____

☐ _____

☐ _____

☐ _____

☐ _____

☐ _____

☐ _____

☐ _____

☐ _____

☐ _____

STEP 5

UNDERSTAND YOUR WEAKNESS

Understand Your Weakness

Have you ever heard the saying, "Your weakness is also your strength?" There is truth in this statement, but people can only gravitate to this concept if they embrace what they believe to be their weakness. Oftentimes, it is easier to pinpoint other people's weaknesses than to acknowledge our own. However, if we truly want to advance in our personal growth and development, we must be willing to embark on a journey of self-discovery. It is important for us to build on the strong parts of our proficiencies, skills, talents, and knowledge while working on the parts that require improvement. When we operate from this level of consciousness, we will understand that our weaknesses and our strengths embody who we are. This acceptance will allow us to be comfortable in our own skin. Identifying and accepting our weaknesses along with our strengths helps to bring more awareness of our true selves.

Our strengths and weaknesses must be in harmony for us to have balance in our lives. If one area is used excessively, this can cause a limitation in our inherent qualities of mind and character, causing us to lose our authentic selves. Personal growth and development start with knowing your strengths and weaknesses and embracing them together, instead of separately. As you do so, you will begin to see yourself as a whole and not in parts and will understand how everything about you completes who you really are. Do not lose the best parts of yourself because you have not mastered your weak parts. You have the power to improve on the weak areas of your life while taking bold steps in the areas where you are strong. Embrace the person you are and look forward to the person you are becoming.

"Sometimes we are tested not to show our weakness,
but to discover our strengths."
—Unknown

Simple in 7 Steps Concept Application

STEP 5

UNDERSTAND YOUR WEAKNESS

It is important to come face to face not only with our best qualities but also with those areas where we may struggle, cover up, suppress, and sometimes feel ashamed to mention. These areas are also important parts of who we are.

What are your strengths?

_____

_____

_____

_____

What are your weaknesses?

_____

_____

_____

_____

How are your strengths and weaknesses connected?

_____

_____

_____

_____

In what ways can you embrace your weakness?

_____

_____

_____

_____

_____

How can you use your strengths to overcome your weaknesses?

_____

_____

_____

_____

_____

What improvement(s) do you need to make in order to obtain your goal?

_____

_____

_____

_____

_____

STEP 6

KNOW WHEN TO QUIT

Know When to Quit

Whether the outcome of life is good or bad, it is filled with plans, assessments, interventions, and revisions. These processes are susceptible to an ebb-and-flow pattern that can lead us into frustration and mental overdrive. The love and passion we have for anything can also become overwhelming. After a while, it can cause a complete depletion of our energy and cause us to lose focus; and can turn into an obsession or preoccupation that ruins the other areas of our lives. The main goal in all aspects of our lives is to have equilibrium. Recognizing when to quit and knowing when to remove ourselves from toxic situations is crucial for our overall well-being. Eliminating the things that prevent growth or cause a distraction should be our number one priority.

A life that is centered, focused, and filled with peace will easily bounce back to the position of stability when circumstances try to disturb its state of balance. If you are involved with any projects, tasks, or relationships that obscure or affect your well-being, you need to take a step back and evaluate their worth. There is nothing wrong with starting over or adjusting your career, businesses, projects, or goals. Sometimes you may have to disconnect from that project or career because of its unfavorable impact on your overall well-being.

To some, you may be viewed as a quitter or unstable because you chose to walk away from that thing, situation, or person that was holding you down. Sometimes, walking away is the only option you have as you seek to achieve eudaimonia in your personal life. There may be great consequences when you make changes in your life. There is a period of adjustment and sometimes a period of fear of the unknown. You may find yourself second-guessing your decision, but keep in mind your "why" and the steps you have laid out to reach your destination. Removing yourself from the things that prevent you from moving forward will increase your potential for personal growth and ongoing success. This is your life's journey, and you control the path it travels on.

> "Sometimes knowing what to do is knowing when to stop."
> –Bill Crawford

Simple in 7 Steps Concept Application

STEP 6

KNOW WHEN TO QUIT

Recognizing when to quit and knowing when to remove ourselves from toxic situations is crucial for our overall well-being. Eliminating the things that prevent personal growth and development should be our number one priority.

What are some signs that would indicate that it is time to quit?

_____

_____

_____

_____

List the advantages and disadvantages of quitting:

PROS	CONS

What is your exit strategy?

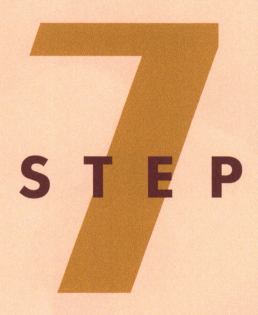

STEP 7

DISCOVER YOUR PURPOSE

Discover Your Purpose

I asked a few of my close friends the question, "How do you know your purpose in life?" One responded immediately, "Look back over your life and see what you do best that brings joy to others, yourself, and glorifies God." Another said, "Identifying your passion and developing it." Our purpose is individualized and unique to each of us. It is an assignment that is innately built to influence those we will touch and transform. Our talents, skills, knowledge, time, etc., are given to us by our Creator to share with others. Sharing these parts of yourself brings a high level of fulfillment, not just to the recipients but also to you.

A purpose-powered life is one filled with cause, provocation, meaning, and aim.

As you discover your purpose and the impact it has on others, you will realize how it aligns with your dreams, values, and actions. You will begin to serve others the parts that bring out the best of you. When you serve others without feeling the need to get paid or rewarded, that is living a purposeful life. Purpose gives you the inspiration and determination to go for what you want in spite of the odds presented before you. It is also the compass that guides you to a life of accomplishment, and satisfaction and has the power to align your outward living with what resides in your heart.

It is never too late for anyone to discover their purpose in life. While you have the right mindset and physical well-being, it is possible. Discovering your purpose is a process that will be revealed over time. Engage in a life that is compassionate toward others, share and do for others, and make a positive impact in the world you live in. Enjoy the journey of your life as you go through the process of discovering your destiny. Learn from your mistakes and from the people who add value to your overall well-being.

"If you can't figure out your purpose, figure out your passion. Your passion will lead you right into your purpose."
—TD Jakes

Simple in 7 Steps Concept Application

STEP 7

DISCOVER YOUR PURPOSE

Purpose gives you the inspiration and determination to go for what you want in spite of the odds presented before you. It is also the compass that guides you to a life of fulfilment, accomplishment, and satisfaction.

When you think of the word "purpose," what comes to mind?

_____
_____
_____
_____
_____
_____

What skills, natural gifts, and talents speak to your purpose?

- _____
- _____
- _____
- _____
- _____
- _____
- _____
- _____
- _____

How does your goal(s) connect with your purpose? List your purpose and the goals that align with them.

PURPOSE	GOALS

What would "fulfilling your purpose" look like? Please describe below.

About the Author

Dr. Jacki Edwards is a published author, inspirational speaker, and board-certified family nurse practitioner. She is the CEO and founder of Jacki Edwards Events & More and How May I Health You, a health coaching company. Her life's story is marked by two failed marriages, unsettling forms of marital abuse, and the struggles of raising children as a single mother. Those periods of lows taught her how to navigate the murky waters of life.

Dr. Jacki has used the steps outlined in her new book *How To Get Your Life In Order By Ordering Your Life's Steps* to bring about change, stability, and financial freedom in her own life. Those hard times also brought her to bended knees, and over the years, she developed a deep, unwavering relationship with her God. Today, she is stronger, wiser, and more confident in who she is and who God wants her to be. Her purpose is to show the manifestation of God in all the areas of her life. The steps she has taken were influenced by her daily communication with God and trusting His leading. Her message conveys reassurance that God is indeed in the affairs of men and that there is a plan and hope-filled purpose for everyone to achieve.

Citation Page

Do you make conscious or unconscious decision? (2014, February 7). Change Factory. https://www.changefactory.com.au/our-thinking/articles/do-you-make-conscious-or-unconscious-decisions/

Goodreads. (2022, September 19). Anthony Robbins Quote. Retrieved from Goodreads: https://www.goodreads.com/quotes/178172-it-is-in-your-moments-of-decision-that-your-destiny

Goodreads. (2022, September 19). Steve Jobs Quote. Retrieved from Goodreads: https://www.goodreads.com/quotes/1259835-don-t-let-the-noise-of-other-s-opinions-drown-out-your

Goodreads. (2022, September 19). Rumi Quote. Retrieved from Goodreads: Let yourself be silently drawn by the strange pull of what you really love. It will not lead you astray

Goodreads. (2022, September 19). Brian Tracy Quote. Retrieved from Goodreads: https://www.goodreads.com/quotes/8723826-be-a-lifelong-student-the-more-you-learn-the-more

Unknown. (2022, September 19). Quotespedia. Retrieved from Quotespedia: https://www.quotespedia.org/authors/u/unknown/sometimes-were-tested-not-to-show-our-weaknesses-but-to-discover-our-strengths-unknown/

Quotefancy. (2022, September 19). Bill Crawford Quotes. Retrieved from Quotefancy: https://quotefancy.com/quote/1702017/Bill-Crawford-Sometimes-knowing-what-to-do-is-knowing-when-to-stop

Goodreads. (2022, September 19). T.D. Jakes Quotes. Retrieved from Goodreads: https://www.goodreads.com/quotes/636989-if-you-can-t-figure-out-your-purpose-figure-out-your

CPSIA information can be obtained
at www.ICGtesting.com
Printed in the USA
BVHW012301100323
660193BV00014B/147